**Eyes on the
Program to**
      i

"The use of self-control is like the use of a break on a train."

----Bertrand Russell

*By **Tony Roman***

Copyright 2015 by WE CANT BE BEAT LLC

Copyright 2015 by Tony Roman.

Published by WE CANT BE BEAT LLC

wecantbebeat.com

Table of Contents

Introduction 5

Chapter One 13

"What am I looking for?" 13

Chapter Two 21

Are you the person you want to be? 21

Chapter Three 40

Put Pen to Paper 40

Chapter Four 49

Are you time Starved? 49

Chapter Five 69

Generating Self-Discipline 69

Chapter Six 83

The Art of Being Positive 83

Chapter Seven 96

Persevere 96

Chapter Eight 103

Conclusion..103

Work Sheet toward greater Self-Discipline.107

Introduction

In today's high tech society we can find an app for just about anything. An app to help us keep track of how many calories we eat, an app to keep track of how many steps we take, and ones like Sworkit that provide high-intensity body weight workouts in case you can't make it to the gym. You would think then that we would have it made today as far as doing just about anything we wanted to. If we want to lose weight, buy an app. If you want to pass a course buy an app. There are even apps on how to become a successful businessman or woman. However, the problem with all of these apps is if you don't have self-discipline you will quit using them, and you will get nowhere. So my friend, how are you going to make yourself keep using these apps so that you can reach the goals you so desire to reach? Say what? You are going to get one of the apps that helps you make your self-discipline stronger? Well good luck with that. What is to prevent you from stopping using that too? Nothing I'm afraid, and that is why you need to read this book.

In this book, *Eyes on the Prize*, you will find some cutting edge ideas that will, if followed, help you finally take control of your life. By showing you how to increase your self-discipline you will be able to do more than you ever thought possible. What is the biggest factor in your life that currently stops you from reaching those goals you are constantly setting for yourself? I bet it is that you lack self-discipline. You find it difficult to do what you need to do for a continued period of time. No need to be ashamed, we all lack self-discipline. Oh yes, we will start a diet, or a class, or maybe even a new hobby, but if you are like me it is not very long before you drop it. What we all lack is self-motivation, which is a big part of self-discipline. Really, who wants to discipline one's self to do those things we really don't like to do in the first place? No one, and if you are like me no one ever taught you how to make your self do these things. Not to worry. This book will teach you everything you need to know to increase you motivation and become more self-disciplined.

If you choose not to read this book and go on with your merry life without learning how to apply self-discipline, you will look back in the future and say to yourself, "I wish I had read that book on self-motivation." I can promise you that you will say this. Why, you ask? Here is why. If you don't learn the basics of self-discipline now, you will probably be doing what other people want you to do, not what you want to, do for the rest of your life. You will wonder why you ended up going to Disney World on Vacation rather than that Casino you had your eyes on. The chances of getting what you want is slight to none unless you have the discipline to make that happen. You will also be eaten up by guilt because you are constantly failing to do those things that are important to you. You did not finish college because you did not have enough self-discipline, and you now weigh over 200 pounds because you had no self-discipline to stop eating or to exercise. As you will see in the future, where you will now be regretting not reading this book, this endless guilt has led to psychological, emotional and physical problems in your life. You will be married to someone who can't help you obtain your full potential because people who lack self-discipline don't attract people with self-discipline. So when you pause and take a look back at your life, you may very well be exhausted, angry and just plain frustrated as to where you are. You most likely will be wondering if reading this book would have made a difference. Let me assure you it will.

Strangely enough, enormous benefits will come from learning self-discipline. The more you learn how to control your wants and desires the greater your *self-confidence* will become. Your *time management skills* will be sharpened like the point on a good knitting needle to the extent that it will seem like you have been awarded more hours in the day. You will not only be able to see results that you have never been able to obtain before, but you will be receiving these results with *less stress and frustration*. Once you follow the steps set out in this book you will see that you are no longer dependent on others to make your goals come true. You will be able to make progress every day toward your goals, because you don't have to depend on others, and in doing so you will pick up a momentum like you have never seen before, and eventually you will become unstoppable. The meaning and fulfillment in your life will reach bounds never before reached and you will have a much more productive, happy, and fulfilled life.

All I am asking you to do is follow the program set forth in this book for 30 days. I bet you did not know that more than three quarters (76%) of people who kept a resolution for thirty days are still following it through a year later! This may seem simple enough, but the statistics also show that 31% of all people who attempted to change a habit, quit within the first 30 days. And believe it or not, a very uninspiring 18% of people reported giving up on their resolutions in the first day.[1]

---

[1] 30 Days of Self-Discipline – The Truth about Tough Change By **Rory Vaden** Published April 10, 2013

Chapter One

"What am I looking for?"

"Man cannot remake himself without suffering, for he is both the marble and the sculptor."

~Dr. Alexis Carrel

Before we can talk about improving our self-discipline it is important that all of us are on the same page as to exactly what self-discipline is. This is important because so many of us have misconceptions about what it is, and if you do not know what it is and you try to conquer it, you are going to fail. The reason you will fail is that many of us think that self-discipline is getting ourselves to like something we need to do. Now, who of us wants to fail? None of us do. So let's make sure we understand what self-discipline is so we don't become disillusioned and then quit our journey to becoming more self-disciplined.

No one wants to discipline themselves. When we think about self-discipline we envision the worse. We see ourselves going through grueling steps to get what we want. Unfortunately self-discipline is getting ourselves to do things we don't like to do, so thinking otherwise is just plain nonsense. If you think self-discipline consists of getting you to like to do things, then you will quit within a couple of weeks when you find out that you have not grown to love dieting, running 5 miles a day or trying to learn a new language. You will be surprised how easily the excuses start popping up if you think that self-discipline is going to make you like something. All of sudden excuses like "My joints are too sore," or "I am too weak when I diet," will start filling up that pretty little head of yours and before you know it you have manufactured several reasons to quit what you have been working on. How surprising that our brain can come up with so many excuses, but then when we want a little self-discipline it totally lets us down. Let me be clear from the start, self-discipline is not making you like to do something that you previously did not like to do, but rather, self-discipline helps us do something over and over again whether we like it or not. It helps us to obtain things we want out of life but are currently unable to obtain because we just don't have the "stick-to-it-ness" that we need to obtain it.

As it is used in this book *self-discipline* will refer to getting yourself to do something on a continuous basis, that you don't enjoy doing. For example, self-discipline will help you study when you don't want to study. It will help you stick with those trombone lessons when you are finding it hard to sit down and practice every day. It won't teach you how to like doing these things, but rather *self-discipline* will provide you with the tools to continue to do these things despite your dislike for them. In a nut shell then, self-discipline involves a set of steps that will help you do those things in life that you should be doing but don't want to be doing. Once you read this book and apply these steps you will be able to get up on time each morning and do the things you want. If your desire is to run in a 5K, as was one of my goals, you will be able to do it once you strengthen your self-discipline. You will pretty much be able to do anything you want to do whether it is something you enjoy or not. Bottom line in life is that you if you want something in life you need to work at it and this requires self-discipline. A basic fact is that sometimes you need to make sacrifices now if you want the prize later.

In the remaining chapters of this book you will learn how to strengthen your self-discipline.

Read each chapter and do the suggested study steps and by the end of 30 days you will be well entrenched with greater motivation empowering you with more self-discipline than you could ever have hoped to dream for. You will learn that not only is self-discipline achievable, but it is also desirable. In chapter two you will begin your journey on this road to self-discipline by first accepting where you currently are, and then determine where you need to go. You will do this by examining your goals. What are your current positive goals, and what negative acts are you doing to prevent yourself from obtaining these goals? By the end of chapter two you will have a set of goals that you are trying to achieve so that later on you can choose one of these goals to work on.

In chapter three you will keep a daily log to determine how you are currently spending your time, and then by looking at how you spend your time each day, you will try to achieve these goals. In chapter four you will take the log you kept in chapter three and analyze it comparing your goals to how you spend your time. The hope here is to discover how you spend your time and to see why it is that the two charts, goals and time, do not seem to match up, i.e. your time chart will show you why you are not achieving your goals.

Chapter five we will explain how to begin a new activity to seek out your goals and will show you when to do it and why to do it then. Couple the advice given in this chapter with the advice given in chapter six as how to remain positive and you will begin to see how, through self-discipline, achieve your goals in life. Chapter six gives you suggestions on how to be positive and to keep working with you goals. And finally chapter seven will explain how to add new activities to your schedule and how to keep doing these activities over and over until they become a habit.

Chapter Two

Are you the person you want to be?

"Who in the world am I? Ah, that's the great puzzle."

--

Lewis Carroll, Alice in Wonderland

So now that you know what self-discipline is and you obviously want to work on yours, let's get started. The first thing you need to realize is that your will power is limited. What I mean by this is that you only have a limited amount of self-discipline each day. If you are using it up all at work, then when you get home it will be more difficult for you to apply it when you are trying to pick healthy food to stay on your diet. So how do you decide what is important in your life? How do you decide what you want to spend your will power on? I bet this never even crossed your mind that we need to make decisions like this. So let me ask you what made you want to work on your self-discipline in the first place? Is there something you did not get done because you lacked motivation? Or, perhaps you got a bad grade in college or lost a deal at work because you did not have the discipline to get it done. This brings us to the first step that you need to do if you want to strengthen your self-discipline. You need to *analyze your life*. Find out what is most important to you in life. If you don't work on something that is important to you, you won't stick with it. You need to be asking yourself the following questions: What are my goals in life? What do I want to be doing five years from now with my life? Do I know what my current main goals or objectives are at work? What is it that I want to accomplish at the end of my day? It is by working on these goals that you will learn self-discipline and will eventually be able to apply this self–discipline to all areas of your life.

If you don't have goals you won't have a happy future and you will waste time trying to increase your self-discipline. Lack of goals will also mean that you will lack direction in your life and the necessary focus to get anything done during the day. You won't be able to navigate toward self-discipline until you have a clarity of purpose and believe in what you are working towards. Goals are important to have because they guide your decision making. If you don't have good goals, or if you don't have any goals at all, you will not make good choices in your life. Having well-defined goals also enables you to measure you success because you can then determine if you are reaching or fulfilling your goals. The question now becomes how do you set your goals so that you will be able to accomplish them? Reaching your goals simply won't happen by you saying "I wish I can, I wish I can," and then expect for something to happen. Unfortunately life does not work this way. To set goals you must sit down and carefully consider what it is you want to achieve, and then put in a lot of hard work and self-discipline to achieve them. There are many steps between setting your goals and achieving them that you aren't aware of yet, but would help you set your goals. In light of this I will provide you some good sound steps for setting your goals so in the end you will be able to achieve them. I have set these steps out below.

Step One: (Day One): Start to think about what you want: Start to consciously think about your goals for life; ask yourself what it is you want out of life. Ask yourself these questions:

What are my goals in life?

What do I want to be doing five years from now with my life?

Do I know what my current main goals or objectives are at work?

What is it that I want to accomplish at the end of my day?

When you start to think about your goals it is important that they motivate you; in other words, make sure that they are important to you and that you want to achieve them because there is some value in achieving them. If the outcomes of achieving the goals you set down for yourself are not important to you, or perhaps they are irrelevant to your bigger life picture there will be no incentive in reaching them. A key to achieving your goals is to be motivated to achieve them; this motivation will come from what you will get from achieving them. In other words, you need to know that you will receive something for achieving your goals, whether it be better health, a better job, or perhaps a better spouse. After you have thought about your goals for a day, and thought about why you want to achieve those goals, you should move to step two where you further examine your goals.

Step Two: (days Two). Examine your Goals: Any road to greater self-discipline begins with sitting down and having a talk with yourself about what it is that you are trying to accomplish in your life. Ask yourself what it is that you want. Is it a family, a good life, a gold medal winner from the Olympics, to be rich and powerful? Make sure you pick goals that are *measurable* so you will be able to see your improvement. When you set your goals make sure you set ones that that relate to the priorities that are the highest in your life. Focusing on goals that are not of high priority will result in you having far too many goals. If you have too many goals you will not have enough time to devote to each one.

Commitment is also an important factor. Without commitment you will not be able to achieve your goals. For each goal then you should feel a sense of urgency where you have a strong sense of "I must get this done." This will increase the likelihood that you will succeed at what you are trying to do. Without this sense of I must get it done, you place your chances of achieving this goal in jeopardy because it is so easy to put it off. Not achieving your goals will make you frustrated and disappointed which in turn will become de-motivating in and of itself. What will happen is that you will end up in a self-defeating state of mind where you will start thinking that you can't do anything right. This is not conducive to achieving any goals.

To make sure your goal is motivating you need to write down why the goals you listed are important to you. Pretend you are trying to convince a friend why they should set this as their goal. What would you tell them are the benefits of achieving such a goal? If you write this down you can go back and look at this reasoning as to why it is important if you lose interest in the goal or if you start to think it is not worthwhile.

SMART GOALS:

A good way to look at your goals and to decide what goals are important for you to reach is to use the **SMART** mnemonic to set up smart goals.[2] This mnemonic states you should have goals that are **S**pecific, **M**easurable, **A**ction-Oriented, **R**ealistic, and **T**ime-Specific. Try and keep these five criteria in mind as you think about your goals and set the goals you want to achieve. Failure to do so will make it much more difficult for you to achieve the self-discipline you so desire.

Specific Goals

---

[2] http://www.livestrong.com/article/210994-5-steps-to-smart-goal-setting/

Being *specific* about your goals means that you need to break your goals down. For example, if your goal is to go back to school, be more specific. A goal that is more specific would be, "I will apply to three colleges where I would like to go back to school." Another example would be if you wanted to lose weight. Instead of just saying you want to lose weight set a more specific goal. Why not set a goal of losing 2 pounds per week. If you don't set specific goals you will get discouraged and give up on them. My original goal of running a 5K was a good goal, but not one that was quickly attainable considering that I have never run before. Because it was not very specific I further broke it down to getting out for 15 minutes every day and at least walk for that long and eventually try and increases it. Also, the more specific a goal is the easier it is to measure it. Which leads us to the second part of setting goals, have goals that are measurable.

Measurable Goals:

The more specific your goals are the easier it is to measure them. For example, if you take the above goal of wanting to lose 2 pounds a week you could further break this down to "I will only eat desert twice a week." This is pretty easy to measure. Include precise amounts, dates, and so on in your goals so you can measure your degree of success. If your goal is simply defined as "to become more fit" how will you know when you have been successful? Having such a general goal is not going to be helpful. Without a way to measure your success you miss out on the celebration that comes with knowing you have actually achieved something. If you are a relatively sedentary person you cannot expect to go out and run a mile right away. Set a measurable goal. Set your goals small at first. Instead of saying you want to run in a 5K why not set your goal in the beginning to something that can be measurable. For example, why not set your goal as walking a mile and then set up smaller measures in-between to reach. Self-discipline is not something you don't have one day and then the next day you do. It is something where you have to set small goals to begin with and then work on strengthening your self-discipline.

Write your goals down and also when you eat a desert write it down so you can keep track of this. Don't kid yourself and think you can remember what days you ate a dessert and what days you did not. This makes it way too easy for you to say to yourself that you don't remember eating a desert one day and then add another one. This is only cheating yourself and will lead to frustration. Remember your goals must be clear and well-defined; generalized or vague goals are not helpful because they don't provide direction. Goals are there to show you the way. If you make well thought out goals they will become easier to obtain, and you will be happier in the long run. Great goals show you where you want to get in life.

Attainable Goals:

You need to make sure your goals are attainable or you are only setting yourself up for failure. Going back to the two goals mentioned above, losing weight and becoming more fit, you cannot set goals that are unreachable; to do so is only setting yourself up for failure. If you set your goal at losing 7 pounds a week, chances of having enough self-discipline to do this is practically none. Furthermore, it is simply unreasonable to expect to lose this much in one week. Setting such a ridiculous goal and then failing to meet it will only demoralize you and make you want to give up. This will eventually erode at your self-confidence. This is why it is a good idea to set it back to two pounds a week. The same could be said for setting a goal to run a 5K. There is no way you are going to go out and run a 5K if you have been sitting at home all this time. Set a smaller goal to start with, let's say walk around the block. This should be attainable and measurable quite readily. On the other side of the coin you need to make sure you don't set goals that are too easy to accomplish. Reaching and obtaining a goal that is too easy can be anticlimactic. This will result in you being fearful of setting more difficult goals for yourself because you will be afraid that you won't be able to reach them. You need to set realistic, yet challenging goals in order to hit a balance that will allow you to challenge yourself. If you can do this you will eventually develop greater self-discipline and find great personal satisfaction.

Relevant Goals:

Make sure your goals fit with what it is you are trying to obtain in life. Ask yourself what direction do you want your personal and work like to take. Once you have done this you can set goals that are relevant to reaching this direction you want to take. If you keep your goals aligned with your life goals you will be able to concentrate on what it is you need to be doing to get what you want. For example, if you want to be a pilot, then set goals that will help you attain this in your life. If you set goals that have nothing to do with this then you are just wasting your time and your attempts at greater self-discipline will fail.

Time Specific

If your goals are not set up to be accomplished within a certain time limit, you will never be able to measure your ability to achieve them. For example, if your goal is simply to lose two pounds, but you do set a time limit when this is to become accomplished, you will not be in any hurry to do this. You will have no way of measuring your success. If you set a deadline, let's say of one week, at the end of one week when your each this goal you can celebrate and this will serve to strengthen your resolve to continue to reach future goals. This is how you work to increase your self-discipline. Deadlines are important because they exert a sense of urgency that is needed to keep yourself working toward the goal you have set for yourself

Chapter Three

Put Pen to Paper

"Paper is to write things down that we need to remember. Our brains are used to think."

— Albert Einstein

When you have a goal in your head it is not real; writing it down makes it a real and tangible. You have no excuse for forgetting about it. When you write them down use words like "I will lose weight" instead of "I would like to lose weight, The way you write them down has more power and will mean more to you if you write it in terms of being something you will do, no hope to do. The first goal statement has power and you can "see" yourself losing weight, the second statement lacks passion and gives you an excuse if you get sidetracked. Do not write your goals so that they give you a way out. Write them so they are concrete in nature and allow no wiggle room.

By writing out the individual steps, and then crossing each one off as you complete it, you'll realize that you are making progress towards your ultimate goal. This is especially important if your goal is big and demanding, or long-term. Remember, goal setting is an ongoing activity not just a means to an end. Build in reminders to keep yourself on track, and make regular time-slots available to review your goals. Your end destination may remain quite similar over the long term, but the action plan you set for yourself along the way can change significantly. Make sure the relevance, value, and necessity remain high.

Step: Thee: (day three). Write your Goals Down: Make sure your write your goals down. This should include your career, health and family goals as well as any other goals you might have. You need to write them down so you won't forget them. I hear you saying to yourself that you won't forget them, but trust me the research is undeniable, people who write down their goals are 42% more likely to achieve them compared to those who don't write them down. [3] So pull out a piece of paper and make a list of what is important in your life. What do you hope to accomplish? Now I am not saying that this will solve everything, but it sure will go a long way in helping you obtain them. This is the beginning of the process of gaining more self-discipline; you have to start somewhere.

There are several reasons why it is important to write down your goals. First and foremost writing down your goals will help you clarify what it is you want in life. If you don't write

---

[3] 30 Days of Self-Discipline – The Truth about Tough Change By **Rory Vaden**
Published April 10, 2013

them down your end game could be overly ambiguous in your mind. Seeing it on paper and writing what you have thought about will help you crystalize what it is you are hoping to accomplish. Writing them down will also motivate you to take action. Goals are useless if you don't execute them. The first step in executing any goal is to write it down. Writing down your goals is also important because this list will prevent you from becoming distracted by new opportunities. Writing them down will also help you to overcome any resistance to obtaining that goal. You will see that once you write down your goals you will start to feel them. Finally, writing down your goals helps you see how far you have come. In a year of two from now, depending on what your goal is, you can pull out your list and see what you have accomplished. Of course you will be able to see how far you have come.

A Word to the wise

As stated above it is very important in developing self-discipline that you choose goals. Once you pick these goals you need to move on or you will never develop the self-discipline that you are hoping to achieve. Thus, when you set your goals choose realistic ones that you will be able to achieve. If you don't set realistic ones you may end up in an endless loop of going one step forward and two steps backwards. In addition to choosing your goals you must also decide what behavior best reflects your goals and values and to follow that behavior over the emotions of the moment.

One thing to keep in mind when choosing your goals is that you must have a strong desire to achieve them. If you are wishy-washy about your goals you are setting yourself up for failure. You need to start out with your goals "living" in your soul. If there is no strong affinity to achieve these goals then you will most definitely fail. Pick goals that you are passionate about.

After developing this program I went through it myself. Here are the goals I listed when I followed this program for thirty days. I thought about my goals for the first couple of days and came up with this list as my original list of goals I was interested in accomplishing.

--Run Five miles a day/Run in a 5K

--lose weight

--eat breakfast every day

--don't overspend

--less time on social media websites

--help other people more

--go to church every week

--volunteer in my community more

--learn something new

Although these were my original goals I modified them using the suggestions in chapter two and three above. No longer did I have the general goal of just losing weight but I changed it to lose one pound a week. Once I made them more specific and measurable this was my new and refined list. Notice I only set my goals for a month at which that time I will reset them to make more progress.

> --I will walk around the block every day for a week, then run ¼ of the block then walk the rest the second week, the third week I will run ½ the block and walk the rest. The third week I will run ¾ of the block and then walk the rest. The fourth week I will run the full block. I will do this at the same time every day.
>
> --I will lose one pound for the next

four weeks

--I will eat breakfast every day after going out to do my exercise.

Notice I started out with only these three so that I am not overdoing it. If you set too many goals at once you will become overworked and stressed out. This will not be conducive to learning self-discipline. In the step where you pick a goal to work on you will just pick one to begin with. Later on you will add a second one.

Chapter Four

Are you time Starved?

"Take Time to deliberate; but when the time for action arrives, stop thinking and go in."

-- Napoleon Bonaparte

If you are like me and most people, I bet you there are times when you have felt that there simply isn't enough hours in the day. Or perhaps, you thought you really would like to spend more time with friends, practicing that new guitar of yours, or going to the beach, but you don't have the time. **Why is it that so many of us feel time-challenged, never having enough time to do the things we want? The main reason for this is that we are not self-disciplined and we are easily distracted by**

all that is going on in the world. A job that might have taken us only an hour turns into a three hour job because we are concentrating on everything but the task at hand. For example, you sit down to work on a paper for school and do everything but that paper. We check our email, we decide to go for a run, or perhaps watch some television, and then we wonder why two hours after we have sat down to write the paper we only have the title page done. We need to become more disciplined in doing these things so that we don't waste our time. The frustrating thing is that when we are younger we have no clue that we are wasting so much time nor do we think logically about the other things we are doing that are getting in the way of us finishing the important tasks we need to do. I know even at my age I had no clue as to how much time I was wasting on nonproductive tasks. This brings us to step number four, tracking your use of time.

Once you choose what goals you want to work on you need to **_track your use of time_**. Don't change anything just yet, but keep a log of what you spend your time on each day. It is important to get a grasp on what exactly we spend our time on. Most of us complain as to how little time in the day we have and wish we could get more done. This is one thing that all successful people have in common. They are self-disciplined enough that they do not waste time. Once you are done with this book you will be able to do the same. Before you try to become more self-disciplined with your time you need to know where you spend your time. The important question here that you are trying to get at is where you are spending your time. Are you spending your time on wasteful projects of perhaps spending too much time with your least important goals? To determine this, follow the time activity log at the end of the book. I bet you don't think you spend much time on non-productive tasks, or ones that provided you little bang for your buck. I can promise you that you will be surprised at just how much time you waste on nonproductive tasks. It is important to keep track of how you are spending your time because you can't make things better unless you know what your base line is. When you properly understand how you use your time at each day, you can minimize or eliminate low value activities. This means that you can do more high value work, while still being able to have time left over for bigger and better things.

<u>Step Four:</u> (Days Four to Five): Keep an Activity Log: Put simply this is a record of how you spend your time. These are sometimes also referred to as a daily activity log, an activity diary or simply as a daily time log. What it basically is, is a written record of how you spend your time. You should do this for two days so as to get an accurate picture of what you do during the day, where you spend most of your time and whether your time is mostly spent on productive tasks. I mean let's face it who would want to be spending most of our days on tasks that are not going to make our life somehow better? By keeping this log for two days you will get a very accurate picture of where all your time goes. Now, let me warn you readers of weak stamina, you are going to be surprised. I know I sure was. I could not believe what an eye-opening experience this was for me. I thought I was pretty adept at allocating my time to important tasks, but once I started writing this down for a couple of days I learned I was not so good, and that rather, I spent way too much time on trivial, nonproductive tasks. No wonder I felt like there was not enough time in the day. (See Index for activity log form).

Not only will this log help you ascertain if you are spending most of your time on unimportant tasks, but it will also show you when you are getting most of your tasks done. Are you more productive at night, first thing in the morning, or maybe in the afternoon? By keeping this log for two days you will be able to see when you are most creative or perhaps the most energetic. Once you determine this you will then be able to apply it to what you do every day. For example, if you find that you are more energetic at nine at night, then this should be when you schedule in your most important work of the day. For those times that you don't perform well or at a higher level, you should schedule less demanding tasks such as returning phone calls or opening your emails. Save your high energy and more focused times for your more important tasks.

Not only are activity logs important for telling us how much time we spend on our critical tasks every day, but they are also useful in helping us identify non-core activities that don't help us meet important objectives. For example, I found that I spent far more time than I thought on Facebook, Instagram and surfing the Internet, or getting coffee each afternoon. When you see how much time you're wasting on such activities, you can then change the way that you work to eliminate them. Part of becoming more self-disciplined is learning to get rid of nonproductive tasks and use that time to complete more productive tasks. I have provided you an activity log in the back of this book. Before you fill it out please read the instructions below.

How to Keep an Activity Log

Please note you should not change your behavior until after you fill out the activity log. You want to be able to evaluate your behavior so as to see where it needs changing. As you look at the activity log you can see that there are five columns that you will need to fill out every time make an entry. The first column is simply the date and time. Every time you are involved in an activity you should note the date and time, a description of the activity, how long the activity lasted and how much value you place on the activity. Make sure that every time you change an activity, whether it is something as simple as getting something to drink, checking your email, or taking time to chat with someone, that you make a note of it. I know these might seem like a big pain and not purposeful at first, but it is important that you do this if you want to strengthen you self-discipline. Not only should you put down what the activity is, but the time of the change and how you feel about it. Feelings include such things as being *tired, excited, energetic, and intense, etc.* When you are finished with this task (or when you have the time to), go back and fill in the rest of the chart, writing down how long the task lasted and how you value the task. When we talk about the value of a task we are referring to how much this task contributes to what you need to be getting done at the time. For example, whether you are studying for an exam, working on a project at work or making dinner for the family, these would be considered important tasks, so you would probably mark these tasks as high intensity ones because they are required to accomplish the goal you are working toward. If you don't study you will fail the exam, if you don't make dinner your family will go without dinner and so forth. If you take time out to get something to drink, you would rank this as a lower quality task because it is not doing something to achieve a bigger goal. Another example of a feeling you might be experiencing is sadness at having to do the task. Whatever the feeling make sure you mark it down. It is really important that you put down how you are feeling at the time. Make sure you keep this activity log for days four and five of your thirty day program to self-discipline. Once you have finished keep the log you need to move onto the next step and analyze it.

Step Five: **(days six & Seven). Analyze your Daily log:**

Learning from Your Activity Log

Once you have kept your activity log for days three and four you need to turn to analyzing it on day five. Don't be alarmed if you find out that you spend considerably more time on jobs that you consider low value. The purpose of this exercise is to determine how you are spending your time. Are you spending it wisely or is too much of your time spend on low level tasks that aren't advancing you and your goals? Other items to look for on you log are those times where you labeled yourself as energetic. These are the times of the day you want to hone in on and assign those tasks that are going to move you forward toward your goals. Being at your best, measured in terms of those times where you are feeling energetic, will help you complete your important tasks more efficiently. It is important to note that sometimes your amount of energy when you are performing a task is not totally dependent on the task but such things as what you are eating and the number of breaks you are taking. Once you've analyzed your Activity Log, you should be able to boost your productivity and eventually self-discipline by applying one of the following actions to various activities:

Eliminate those tasks or actions that are not germane to you accomplishing your goals, or those which don't help you meet your objectives. If you find yourself spending too much time watching television and not getting your work done you need to eliminate some, if not all of it, until it no longer gets in your way of accomplishing your daily tasks and eventually your long term goals. If there are tasks you are doing, that need to be done, but are still getting in the way of you successfully completing your goals, find ways to either shorten the time it takes to complete the task or see if you can get someone else to complete the task for you. Learn to delegate said tasks to someone else in the family or hire someone to do them.

A Second thing you should be doing is teasing out of your daily log when your energy levels are the highest. Remember how you were asked to put down how you felt when you completed your tasks? Go back and check when these times occurred for you and use these times to schedule your most challenging daily tasks. If you perform you most challenging tasks when your energy levels are the highest your work will be of a much higher quality. What you are doing here is finding your optimum times to do tasks. In addition to your high energy time look for how often you are switching tasks.

Another piece of data you should be able to extricate from your daily log is how often you are switching from one type of task to another? If you are checking emails four times a day and doing other tasks in between you would do much better to check and reply to your emails only once or twice a day. Try to reduce the number of times you are switching tasks and you will become more productive.

Step Six: (Days eight and Nine): Research the area in which you are lacking control:

Once you figure out what area you're weak in you should do some research so you can have a better understanding of what it is you are having trouble with. Read articles, books and blogs if any exist on the areas you are having difficulty with. The more informed you become the easier it is to make the right decision when you're tempted to overdo something. For example if you are wanting to learn to run and have never done it before, take time to read up on the proper equipment needed for this, proper warm up exercises, how to run and how to cool down when you are done. Find out if there are any types of foods you should be eating that may give you an edge. See if you can find a set of instructions on how to work up to the five miles you are hoping to eventually run. You won't be able to start running five miles the first day so you will need a plan. If you cannot find it on the internet don't hesitate to go to the library.   As you will eventually figure out, the more you learn about what you are trying to do the more motivated you will become, and the easier it will be for you to become self-disciplined and accomplish what you want to accomplish. Remember that in terms of gaining self-control, knowledge really is power! You will also find that friends with similar problems or desires will be a big help to you. If you can get them to share their experiences with you, you can then compare and contrast strategies you are using, or considering using. Finding a person with the same goal as you will be reassuring in that will know that you are not the only one with the need for more self-discipline; in summary this tells you that you are not a weak person. On the contrary it tells you that you are ahead of the game in that you are seeking out your own solutions to your problem.

Chapter Five

Generating Self-Discipline

"We are what we repeatedly do, excellence then is not an act, but a habit"

~Aristotle

Now that you have crystallized your goals and have looked at how you spend your times it is time to take action.   I am sure you are wishing you could just snap your fingers and just get what you want at this point, but as far as self-control goes, this does not work. You do have the power to change but it will take a little more time. This step involves you picking out your best time each day. You should know this now from your daily log you have kept. Take this time and choose this as the time you are going to start your new behavior. Now you don't want to overdo so you will do your new behavior for fifteen minutes during this time. It is not important that you complete this task in this time, but that you do this behavior at this time every day for the next ten days. The object here is to begin to make this new task a habit. The more you do something on a continual basis, the greater chance of it becoming a habit. And as we all know habits are difficult to get rid of. The problem is that most of us cultivate bad habits, not good ones. Your aim here is to take those things you want to accomplish and make them a habit.

<u>Step Seven</u>: Take Action (days 10 thru day 30) – For the next week you are to perform the behavior you have chosen at this precise time that you have discerned is the best time of the day for you. You are to do it for only fifteen minutes and don't concentrate on whether you finish it, but just concentrate on doing it every day and this time for an entire week.   For me I chose to start my running then. Now of course since I had never been running before I did not accomplish much in fifteen minutes, but every day I was out there from 8 AM to 8:15 AM trying to run. It was no big accomplishment as far as I thought but when I look back on the days I started doing this and kept doing it for an entire week I am quite impressed. The reason being is that I had never run before in my life. Now, for an entire week I was out there running, walking, running, walking until and the end of a week I was doing more running than walking. The most important thing was that I stuck with it for a whole week. There are several things you can do to help yourself keep motivated so that you can stick this out and not quit. If you don't you will fail at establishing self-discipline.   You need to get back on that horse.

Accountability Partner

Sometimes it helps if you have someone else to report to, to help you maintain your goals. This will help you remain productive and to keep you on track toward your goals. Ask a spouse, friend or peer to be you accountability partner. If you do this make sure you share the goals you set down for yourself and outline your expectations for your progress. It will also be useful to share your specific goals and how you plan on measuring them. Meet with your accountability person at least once a week. Often times we are more likely to do what we have set up for ourselves if we are going to let someone down besides ourselves. We are less apt to disappoint someone else than we are ourselves. This just might be the spark you need to keep you doing this behavior at the time you set up for yourself each day.

Another good option to help you is if you can find someone who has a similar goal who is willing to pursue your goal with you. I was very lucky to have someone who already was into running and who met me each day to run with me. He was such a great coach. He was way ahead of me when it came to running when it came to running because he was a former marine. But he stood by me and encouraged me every day. He stood there and cheered me on in my endeavor to make it around that block every day. He praised me for doing well and when I was struggling he cheered me on to do more.

The Magic of Four Days

If you are intent on becoming more self-disciplined it is paramount that you do your new behavior for four days straight without missing a day. If you can do this you are on your way to making this a habit. Yes, four days are the magic number of days. If you can do your first goal four days straight you have it made. For example, as one of the goals I had, eating breakfast every day, I did not skip eating breakfast for four days. Guess what, after that it became much easier. The same thing with my goal of walking around the block every day. I made it through the first four days and then it got easier. We can handle taking a two day break, even three days, we often take a three way weekend but when we take any more than this off from our routine it is much harder to get back into your daily routine. When you extend it more than three days it becomes a pattern. Notice how different it feels when you return to work after a three day weekend versus a four day weekend. It is so much more difficult to get back into the swing of things. Although it is only a difference of one day it makes a big difference. So goes the power of the four day rule. If you want something as a habit do it for four days straight and you are on your way to making it a habit. It is important to remember if you break this rule not to quit. It is not that you can't make it a habit if you have not done it four days straight, it is just a little harder to do so. **Kicking yourself around and getting all depressed if you have missed four days straight of doing your goals will only use**

up your good energy and will take away attention and time you could be using to get re-establish a pattern of behavior. If you skip days, then go to the next rule of thumb: Get back on your horse as soon as possible. The sooner you bet back into your habit the better off you will be. Don't put off until tomorrow what you can do today.

Are you having a hard time getting started?

If you are having a hard time acting on your goal or sticking with it, take a step back and ask yourself this question. Is this a goal I really want? Is this something you really want, or is this something you think others want for you? If this is something the rest of the world is telling you should want but you don't want it, you will never take action on it. You can't really want something just because other people want you to have it. If you are doing this you are wanting a goal by "proxy." This means that you only want a goal because you think it is what everyone else wants for you. If you are having trouble acting on your goal and you think it might be because it is a goal by "proxy" ask yourself the following questions.

> Do you think others will think differently if you decided not to pursue this goal?

> Do you think you should want this goal?

> Do you feel guilty if you don't want this?

Do your friends/ role models say you should want this?

Do your friends/family/ role models want this for themselves?

Did someone else assign this goal to you?

Answering yes to any of the above question indicates that this may not be a goal you really desire to achieve. It is more than a good chance that you are attempting to achieve this goal because you think it is what others want.

A second reason you might be having a hard time getting started with your goal or inability to keep doing your goal each day is that you have set this goal because you did not know what else to set. This is not a very effective way to choose a goal. If you are setting a goal just because you don't have clarity as to what you want as a goal, this will not work either. Things you should be asking yourself to determine if this is the case are does removing this goal make me feel lost or fearful or confused? Did you select this goal when you were panicky or anxious? Finally, if you remove this goal would you have to do some real soul searching to find a new goal? Once again if you answered yes to any of these questions you need to find a better goal for yourself.

Finally, if you are having trouble getting started with your goal you need to examine if this is a goal you really want now, right this minute, not something you wanted in the past. Questions that will help you determine if this is the case are if you were to wake up tomorrow with amnesia and had to set a new goal would this be one you set. Another question to ask yourself to find out if this is a current goal for you if the circumstances are the same for you as when you first set this goal. Also do you ever forget about this goal and has your vision changed since you made this goal. If you answer yes to any of these questions maybe this is an old goal and not a goal you should be currently trying to fulfill.

What if I set a wrong goal?

So, to recap what I have just said. If you have a difficult time getting active on your goal you should evaluate your goal and see if this is a goal you really want. Ask yourself the above questions to ascertain why you set this goal. If you find that you set it for any of the above reasons then you should stop pursuing that goal, it is not one you really want. If it is not a goal you want you **might consider a different version of the goal or a specific part of the goal that may fit you.** Ask yourself what about that goal resonates with you, if anything. You might also want to scarp the goal entirely and start with a new one. The bottom line is that if you have not worked toward the goal you originally chose it means you don't really want the goal. Find one that you really want and then get working on that one.

Chapter Six

The Art of Being Positive

"There are two primary choices in life: to accept conditions as they exist, or accept the responsibility for changing them."

-Denis Waitley

By now you should be feeling well on your way to accomplishing your goal. I know you may think that doing something for just fifteen minutes a day is not much and won't get you very far, but step back and think about it. When was the last time you ever have done anything at all for an entire week in a row? If you have been lacking self-discipline, your answer to this is probably either never, or so long ago you can't remember. I was so proud of myself that I got out there every day and tried to run. I must admit at first I could barely walk for the entire block that I picked out to do this around, but I kept with it. At first I would run for maybe five or six steps, then I would walk and I would try to run again. It went slow the first couple of days but by the end of the week I was running for at least half of the fifteen minutes. Believe it or not I could actually see improvement. Part of what made me keep with it was attaching something that I liked to do with this new behavior that I was trying to establish. The object here is to take something you do every day and attach it to your new behavior. I bet you are asking yourself how this could ever work. I was a little skeptical in the beginning too, but I thought oh, what the heck let's give it a try.

Step Eight: (days 10 to 30) add a positive habit:

At first I was at a loss as to what to add to my task of jogging. Then it dawned on me. I loved to take the dog for a walk so why don't I just make this her walk time? So half way during the week of doing my first task I starting bringing the dog with me. I had to walk the dog and I loved to do is so now I was associating something I liked with something I was trying to make myself do. Yes, it was so much easier to get up every day and take my dog for a walk. My brain associated this with a positive feeling. Now when I did both together I was making my brain share the positive feeling I was getting from walking the dog and also associating this good feeling with jogging. I was teaching my brain to associate a good feeling with jogging. It was learning to replace the negative feeling I was having with jogging with the positive feeling from walking the dog. I was surprised how this really did occur; the more I walked the dog while I was trying to run or jog, the more my brain started to tell me it liked this new activity. It was totally amazing. My dog loved the extra attention and quite frankly was surprised that her mom had it in her to run. I actually started looking forward to that fifteen minutes every day as the dog and I head out to run. To further strengthen my resolve I started using another technique also, the technique of positive feedback, or positive thinking.

Step Nine: (days 7 to 30) Work on Positive Thinking: I found that in order to keep myself going and on an upbeat path, that it was good to work on my positive thinking. Like anything, how we think can be something we can work on. We can learn to change our thinking to something more helpful and this is what I concentrated in doing. What I found is that once I started thinking more positively it was easier to do things that were good for me to do. It helped me want to do things to. What you should do in this step is every day write down one sentence to yourself that you would tell a friend who was trying to accomplish the same things you are trying to accomplish. In my case I would write things like, "You are strong, and you can do this." Each day I would write one of these statements and hang them somewhere I would be able to see them throughout the day. I took a piece of colored cloth and hung it up on the wall at the head of by bed where I could read them. You can hang them on your bathroom mirror, your refrigerator or anywhere you can view them every day and throughout the day. Other one sentence notes I would write to myself included things like, "You go can do this," and "Wow, look how far you have come." Be positive and act like you are writing to your friend. For some reason we are always nicer to our friends, but remember you are your own best friend. Write yourself some great positive sentences of encouragement and keep repeating those sentences over and over every day. I have listed several steps you can take to help yourself remain a positive thinker.

1. *The past does not equal the future*: People do not have a run of bad luck, there is no such thing. What has happened in the past does not mean this will happen in the future and you need to stop thinking that it will. If things did not go well for you at last night's class, this doesn't mean everything else will go wrong. If you did bad on the exam don't give up or assume that this is how you will do in the future.

This will quickly pull you away from your quest for self-discipline.

2. *Do not permit self-fulfilling prophecies*: If you believe that the rest of your night will go like your exam went, then rest assured you will either do or say something to make your predication come true. Put a stop to this type of thinking immediately. Take the one bad test grade at face value, it is just one bad grade and it is not a sign of things to come. Don't think this way.

3. *Look at the big Picture*: Unless it is some life changing event like a major car

accident or a death in the family chances are you will forget whatever happened in two weeks or less. If you don't meet your goal one day you need to keep on keeping on, don't let this get you down. In two weeks you won't even remember what went wrong. Don't blow things out of proportion.

4. *Change your level of Irritation:* Start looking at good days as any day you aren't not drowning and your head is above water. Make bad days only those days where you house burns down or your car rolls into the river. You can define good and bad for yourself. Do this with your

goals and your self-discipline. Any day you keep to your goals is a good day and should be looked upon as such.

5. *Take Care of yourself:* You need to remember that your brain has a lot to do with how you feel. If you feed your brain negativity it will spit out negativity. Your brain and body are constantly in touch with each other sending messages back and forth. If you don't take care of your body your brain is not going to feel better. It is important that you eat properly and exercise. Bad moods will make you tired, try to overcome this by getting up and exercising. The more you keep your body

and brain at optimal functioning the better you will do at achieving self-discipline. The minute you let your negative attitude take over the harder it will be to become more self-disciplined.

6. *Keep your eye on the prize:* Don't concentrate on those things that are going wrong. Keep your eye on the prize and concentrate on all those things that are going right. This will help you do more right and not succumb to the bad or that little voice telling you, "You blew it no sense keeping up with those goals now" Go back to bad you don't need to run today. Or it is OK to have that piece of

cake. Never mind these voices. Stop them before they start by looking at the positive that is going on around you. There is always plenty of that to follow. To help you do this make a list of the good things going on in your life and post it somewhere where you will see it often.

7. *Expect only the best:* As my mom always used to say, "You get what you expect to get." In other words if you act like everything is gloom and doom then expect to get that in your life. The attitude you go around with is what you will attract. If you act like wonderful things will happen to you and expect the best you have a

much better chance of obtaining the best. When you are striving for self-discipline don't act like it is hard to obtain. Keep a positive attitude and expect the best from life.

Chapter Seven

Persevere

"It doesn't matter if you try and try and try again, and fail. It does matter if you try and fail, and fail to try again."

~ Charles Kettering

If you are going to achieve anything in life you can't stop with just making just one change. It is important that you add another and do this for a period of time also. If you don't start adding other activities that will lead toward your goal you will stagnate and not move forward.

Step Ten: (days 10 to 30) add a second task:

When you reach day 10 it is time to add a second task to your routine. It does not have to do with the first task, or it could. This is up to you. Do what you did with your first activity. Go to your activity log and analysis of it and locate another time when you are high functioning and ad your second task to this time. Once again only do this task for fifteen minutes a day at that time. Whether you are done or not quit after fifteen minutes. By this time I was getting so excited about the running I added a second time of the day devoted to running. I must admit I was finding this quite enjoyable. Not only was I able to run more and more the longer I stuck with it, but I was meeting some of my other goals also. I was starting to lose weight. I took my dog with me each time I spent the fifteen minutes in the morning and the fifteen in the afternoon running. As I said when I first began I could not even make it around the entire parking lot running. I had to walk most of it at first and then the more I did this the greater distance I could run.

You might find it challenging to sustain your enthusiasm for keeping with your goals, but don't give up. Here are some suggestions as how you can keep your enthusiasm fresh and alive. Try picturing the resolution and don't concentrate on the struggle you are having. Visualize you overcoming the challenge and keep you mind on the success of doing what it is you want to do. To help yourself do this minimize the amount of stress you are undergoing. To do this eat right, exercise and get the right amount of sleep. If you are stressed you will only focus more on your struggles and have a more difficult time overcoming them. You don't want to put a damper on your enthusiasm so do your best to minimize the amount of stress you have. Also, the less stress you have the easier it will be to stay focused. Staying focused allows you to maintain a higher level of enthusiasm. The greater you level of enthusiasm the better you will do at staying focused and keeping with your goals. Remember that the important thing here is to stick with your goals so you can build up your self-discipline. You will strengthen your self-discipline by learning how to formulate your goals and then following this plan to stick with them. Self-discipline is a tool for helping you do what you want in life. This plan, if you persevere will work for any goals you have. It is just important to make the actions you are taking to achieve these goals part of a habit. It is by making them a habit that you will increase you self-discipline.

Other things that will help you reach your goals and increase your self-discipline is to keep things *fresh*. Don't let your life fall into a stagnant pattern. If this happens you will be facing an even bigger struggle. You can keep your enthusiasm high by practicing fresh thinking.

Always try and think of new and exciting things you can do to increase your chances of obtaining your goals. Avoiding procrastination will also go a long way in helping you reach your goals. Keep moving and keep an eye open for any procrastination that may be creeping up on you. If you notice this happening take action to get your enthusiasm back. Strive to keep an open mind allowing new ideas to enter you mind so you can contemplate using them in you struggle to obtain more self-discipline. Finally, don't sweat the little things. Whereas you might be faced with small setbacks don't let these little setbacks get in your way. That's all they are, little setbacks. They won't matter in the long run and this is what you need to remember.

It is important to remember that your greatest feeling of success comes from conquering these struggles you face. You will feel much pride and satisfaction when you overcome these obstacles and reach the goals you set out to achieve. Remember if you keep your eyes on the prize the satisfaction will be ten-fold when you achieve success. Your success will be ever so much sweeter when you have overcome the obstacles that you have met on the way. Hang in there and success and greater self-discipline will be yours.

Chapter Eight

Conclusion

"Success is not final, failure is not fatal: it is the courage to continue that Counts."

-Winston Churchill

My hope for you in writing this book was to give you a chance at obtaining self-discipline like I did. At one time in my life I was struggling with little to no self-discipline and became aware that

I was not getting what I wanted out of life. Because of lack of self-discipline I had put on a fairly large amount of weight, had found in hard to study at school and had just about given up on getting those things I wanted in life. All of these "failures" led to a very bad view of who I was and what I was all about. I felt useless, fat, ugly and just plain dumb. Then one day, I am not exactly sure what struck me, but I came up with a plan to start getting what I wanted. The one thing I wanted the most at that time was to lose weight. I figured if I could do this I could then do anything. So I started my program as explained in this book. As I stated is was slow going in the beginning and I could not see my way to the end, but as the program suggest all you need to do is start with fifteen minutes a day, every day for a week. I did this and then added a second fifteen minute time period. I put a fun habit or activity to these time slots and before I knew it I was enjoying running. Matter of fact I eventually got up to 10 miles a day and got to run in that 5K I wanted to. The more I ran the more I liked it; something I never thought I would be able to say. I was never very athletic but this program did it for me. It gave me the discipline I needed to run each day. I even ended up losing over 100 pounds after one year. This success can be yours too. Just read this book, follow the steps and you will increase you self-discipline beyond what you ever thought possible. You don't need to stop with just one goal but once you learn self-discipline anything can be yours. The sky is the limit once you read this book and learn how to discipline yourself.

Work Sheet toward greater Self-Discipline

Step One: (Day One): Start to consciously think about your goals for life; ask yourself what it is you want out of life.

Step Two: (Day Two): Make a rough list of what it is you are wanting to accomplish in your life. Ask yourself what you would like do differently. Consider health, social, economic or any other area you would like to achieve. Write your rough list before.

_____

_____

Step Three: (Day three): Pick out three or four of your main goals from the list above and write them below as your final list of goals.

_____

_____

_____

Step Four: (Day Four thru Six): Fill out the following activity log

                          Daily Activity Log

Date/Time	Activity	How I feel	Duration	Value (H,M,L)

<u>Step Five:</u> (days seven thru eight): Analyze your Daily log

<u>Step Six</u>: (Day Nine thru Ten): Research the area in which you are lacking control

Step Seven: (days 10 thru day 17): Take Action

Step Eight: (days 10to 30) Add a positive habit

Step Nine: (days 10 to 30) Work on Positive Thinking:

Step Ten: (days 10to 30) Add a second Task

Printed in Great Britain
by Amazon